Animals on the Farm

Sheep

Megan Kopp

Go to **www.av2books.com**, and enter this book's unique code.

BOOK CODE

K487690

AV² by Weigl brings you media enhanced books that support active learning.

AV² provides enriched content that supplements and complements this book. Weigl's AV² books strive to create inspired learning and engage young minds in a total learning experience.

Your AV² Media Enhanced books come alive with...

Audio
Listen to sections of the book read aloud.

Video
Watch informative video clips.

Embedded Weblinks
Gain additional information for research.

Try This!
Complete activities and hands-on experiments.

Key Words
Study vocabulary, and complete a matching word activity.

Quizzes
Test your knowledge.

Slide Show
View images and captions, and prepare a presentation.

... and much, much more!

Published by AV² by Weigl.
350 5ᵗʰ Avenue, 59ᵗʰ Floor
New York, NY 10118
Website: www.av2books.com   www.weigl.com

Library of Congress Cataloging-in-Publication Data

Kopp, Megan.
 Sheep / Megan Kopp.
   p. cm. -- (Animals on the farm)
 Includes index.
 ISBN 978-1-61913-278-8 (hard cover : alk. paper) -- ISBN 978-1-61913-282-5 (soft cover : alk. paper)
 1. Sheep--Juvenile literature. I. Title.
 SF375.2.K67 2013
 636.3--dc23
                          2011049158

Printed in the United States of America in North Mankato, Minnesota
1 2 3 4 5 6 7 8 9 0 16 15 14 13 12

022012
WEP020212

Project Coordinator: Aaron Carr   Art Director: Terry Paulhus

Weigl acknowledges Getty Images as the primary image supplier for this title.

Animals
on the Farm

Sheep

CONTENTS

3

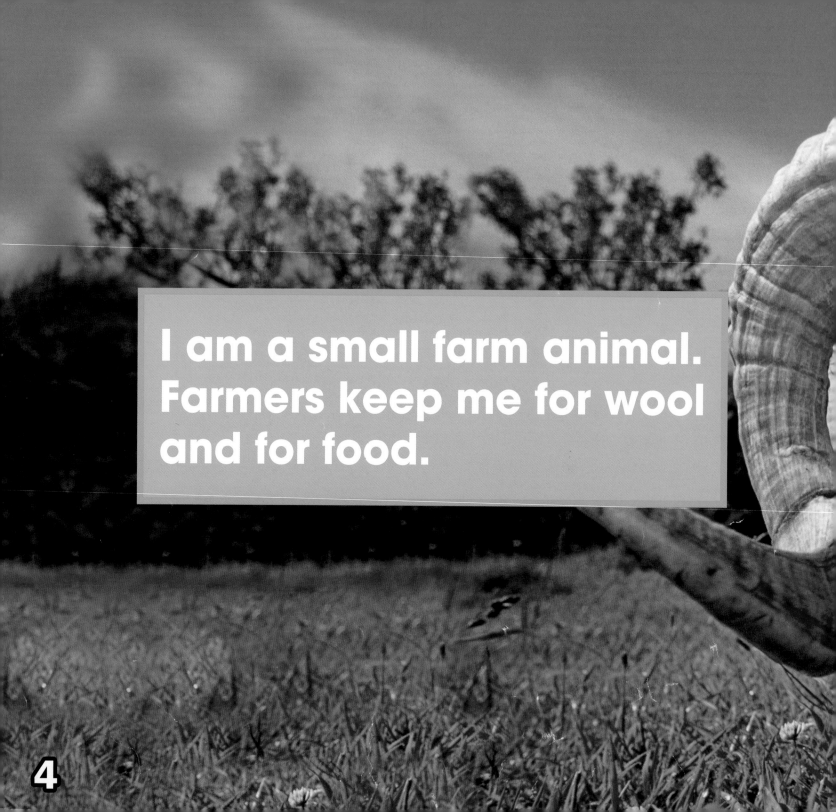

I am a small farm animal. Farmers keep me for wool and for food.

4

5

I am a mammal. I have fur called fleece all over my body.

I use my four strong legs to jump, run, and walk. My feet are called hoofs.

My fleece keeps me warm.
My fleece can also
keep people warm.

I eat grass and other plants.
I chew my food and swallow.
Then I bring my food back up
and chew it again.

I say hello with a "bahhh."
This is called bleating.

15

I like being with other sheep.
My group of sheep
is called a flock.

17

I give birth to one or two babies at a time.

My babies are called lambs.

My lambs learn to walk
a few hours after being born.

21

SHEEP FACTS

These pages provide more detail about the interesting facts found in the book. They are intended to be used by adults as a learning support to help young readers round out their knowledge of each animal in the Animals on the Farm series.

Pages 4–5

Farmers keep sheep for their wool. Farmers shear their sheep each spring. Shearing does not hurt. The fleece is cut off, cleaned, and spun into wool. Most sheep have white fleece, but it can also be black, gray, silver, brown, or red. The fleece from one sheep can be spun into a strand of wool 124 miles (200 kilometers) long.

Pages 6–7

Sheep are mammals. This means their bodies are covered in hair and they give birth to live young. Baby mammals drink milk from their mother's body. Male sheep are called rams. Female sheep are called ewes. Sheep have long muzzles, pointed ears, and some have horns. Sheep have excellent senses of hearing, eyesight, and smell. There are more than 200 breeds of sheep.

Pages 8–9

Sheep have four feet called hoofs. Sheep have four slim but strong legs. They have cloven-hoofed feet. This means that their hoofs are divided into two toes. Like ballerinas, sheep jump, run, and walk on their toes.

Pages 10–11

A sheep's fleece keeps it warm. Fleece can be long and coarse or short and fine. When farmers cut off a sheep's fleece, it is called shearing. Farmers shear their sheep once each year. The fleece, or wool, is used to make items such as clothes and blankets. One sheep produces 8 to 10 pounds (3.6 to 4.5 kilogram) of wool each year.

Pages 12–13

Sheep chew all of their food twice. Sheep graze for about seven hours each day. They eat plant material found close to the ground. Their food includes grass, clover, weeds, leaves, and twigs. Sheep are ruminants, with four parts to their stomach. They chew and swallow their food. Then, they spit up the food to chew it again.

Pages 14–15

Sheep talk to other sheep by bleating. A baby sheep knows its mother by her bleat. Sheep are usually quiet, but they will bleat if they are hungry, afraid, or trying to get another sheep's attention. Often, sheep will bleat when they are about to be fed.

Pages 16–17

Sheep like being with other sheep. Sheep are social animals. They stay in large groups called flocks. It is rare to see a sheep by itself. Flocks also provide protection from predators, such as mountain lions, coyotes, and wolves. Sheep also like to be around people. People that care for sheep are called shepherds.

Pages 18–19

Sheep often have babies in the spring. Their babies are called lambs. Ewes have a 147-day, or five-month, gestation period. They give birth to one to three babies. Usually, ewes give birth to one lamb. For the first few weeks, lambs need to drink their mother's milk every one to two hours. Lambs can sleep up to 12 hours a day.

Pages 20–21

Sheep can have more than one baby at a time. Lambs can weigh 8 to 10 pounds (3.6 to 4.5 kg) at birth. A newborn lamb learns to walk within a few hours of birth. Lambs stay with their mother for five months. Full-grown sheep can weigh up to 400 pounds (180 kg). Sheep live for 10 to 12 years.

WORD LIST

Research has shown that as much as 65 percent of all written material published in English is made up of 300 words. These 300 words cannot be taught using pictures or learned by sounding them out. They must be recognized by sight. This book contains 50 common sight words to help young readers improve their reading fluency and comprehension. This book also teaches young readers several important content words. These words are paired with pictures to aid in learning and improve understanding.

Page	Sight Words First Appearance
4	a, am, and, animal, farm, food, for, I, keep, me, small
6	all, have, my, over
8	are, feet, four, run, to, use, walk
11	also, can, people
12	again, back, eat, it, other, plants, then, up
15	is, say, this, with
16	being, group, like, of
18	at, give, one, or, time, two
21	after, few, learn

Page	Content Words First Appearance
4	farmers, wool
6	body, fleece, fur, mammal
8	hoofs, legs
12	grass
15	bleating
16	flock, sheep
18	babies, birth
19	lambs
21	hours

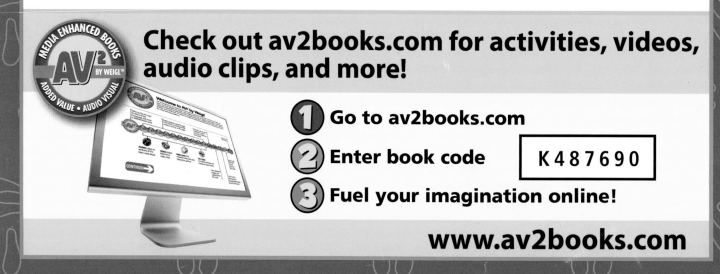

Check out av2books.com for activities, videos, audio clips, and more!

1 Go to av2books.com

2 Enter book code   K 4 8 7 6 9 0

3 Fuel your imagination online!

www.av2books.com